The Mackerel at St. Ives

D1603026

The Mackerel at St. Ives

Poems by Arthur Brown

David Robert Books

Published by David Robert Books
P.O. Box 541106
Cincinnati, OH 45254-1106

ISBN: 9781934999325
LCCN: 2008938623

Poetry Editor: Kevin Walzer
Business Editor: Lori Jareo

Visit us on the web at www.davidrobertbooks.com

For Poem,
our two fathers, our two mothers,
and Dmitri and Sadie

Acknowledgments

Blue Unicorn: "Still Life," "The Stripèd Lion"
Dogwood: "On Leash," "Swing"
The Evansville Review: "The Chinese Princess Tree,"
    "The Hitchhiker"
The Formalist: "The Carny," "The Balloon-Blower,"
    "The Mailbox," "Major American Authors I," "An
    Old Photo on Today's Front Page," "Premonition,"
    "Theresa" "A Voice Out of the Blue"
The Ledge: "On Seeing Monster's Ball"
The Malahat Review: "Identification," "Notes for the
    Rabbi's Eulogy"
Michigan Quarterly Review: "Prophecy"
Measure: "After Death," In the L.A. Half-Light,"
    "Diamond"
Poetry: "Private Showing"
The Southwest Review: "The Tomb of Hunting and
    Fishing" (Winner of the 2005 Morton Marr Poetry
    Prize, selected by William Logan)

"Jackson Square, New Orleans" was the Winner of the
2007 Nebraska Shakespeare Festival Anne Dittrick Sonnet-
Writing Contest.

"Premonition" was reprinted in *Sonnets: 150 Contemporary
Sonnets,* ed. William Baer (University of Evansville Press,
2005)

Many thanks to the editors of these publications. Special
thanks to Bill Baer, Andy Davis, and other good friends
and readers.

Table of Contents

I.

Premonition

A sort of surfacing it seemed to be,
as of a fish into the light and air
that for an instant, as it's hanging there,
with a strangely steadfast certainty
takes up the currents of another sphere,
before it drops again into its own—
heavy as a triply skipping stone
that will at last forever disappear.
Five gulls, their calls, the crescent moon and sky
(the gray unearthly white against the blue),
the spirit-sounding things of sea and shore
conjoin to lure my untrained ear and eye
to the endlessness of my own death—
then leave me stranded here to live some more.

Theresa

No child has left me dazed like you just did—
I mean for having grown into adulthood.
"There's no one home but me," you said. And I said, "Things
have changed." That's more than obvious.
We heard you born from just outside the door,
and seeing what sex you were, that all was well,
we ran for beer and brought St. Pauli Girl
into the room itself, and saw you off
within hours—your mother and father a family.
You say you had a summer guest from Spain.
Now you're headed off to Martha's Vineyard.
Tell your dad I'll call him in July.
Tell him I'd like to share a Guinness with him.
And tell your mom I had a dream of her—
we were climbing a snow-covered mountain.
Give our love to Anna, our goddaughter,
and Benjamin, the baby—is he walking?
Hanging up, I pick up crumbs from the floor—
my wife's downstairs, the children upstairs fighting.
It was your manner, remote and understanding,
your portrait-of-a-lady voice and presence,
that's given me this taste of obsolescence.

The Carny

Driving home they stopped in Riverbend—
Ferris wheels and coasters caught their eye.
"Come on, Dad," the carny called him—ghostly,
cross-legged on a crate and leaning back,
smoke- and beer-eyed, mustached, parchment-skinned.
His pretty wife chirped out, "Why don't you try?"
3 Balls to Break 2 Bottles—Millers mostly,
upside down, necks collared in the rack.

"Okay," he said, almost against his will,
moving to one arm their little son;
"I'll try it holding him"—a compromise.
"Nah," the carny said and shook his head,
taking from the wife her dollar bill;
"Mama'll hold the baby till your done"—
then blew out smoke that did its best to rise
genie-like inside the narrow shed.

Shifting thus their burdens: woman—child,
man—three pocked and heavy yellow balls
("Polo balls," it came to him absurdly),
he juggled them five passes just for show,
although the carny wasn't looking. Prizes
watched him: elves and trolls and kewpie dolls,
snakes whose glassy eyes seemed otherworldly—
waiting mutely there for him to throw.

Missing narrowly its mark the first ball

15

slammed into the corrugated tin.
"That's hard enough!" The father's throw impressed him,
slouching in the corner of his den.
Then everybody heard the baby wail.
Mama turned him toward the goldfish bin,
"Papa's trying to break the bottles"—kissed him.
Papa didn't turn and tried again.

The wall resounded like a trashcan drum.
"Oh," the mother said. The carny nodded:
one ball left, the father could not win,
failing there before his little son,
as if the act foreshadowed things to come.
"A dollar'll give you four," the carny prodded,
gambling that the man would not give in.
"Thanks," he said and turned. "I've had my fun."

Swing

Poised atop the arc—not looking down
at any consequence he might have feared,
as if the swing had been more verb than noun
and poles and chains and strap had disappeared,
and in the balance there his very breath
conspiring with the blueness of the sky,
as if he'd gone an instant past his death
so never afterwards would have to die—
he swung, until the downward swing began,
the sentence having once been set in motion
pointing gravely to return the man,
however spirited his upward notion:
kicking out his heels for all he's worth,
the better part of him bent back to earth.

The Stripèd Lion

God I love that, when they ask you for some help—
"Daddy, where's the stripèd lion?" (*stripèd*,
that's how he said it)—and you know and give it—
"You were playing with it in the bath"—
and they say, "Oh," and run and get it, and run
again upstairs to kill the dinosaurs.
The stripèd lion, that's the father in me;
the tiger is the man they've yet to meet,
hunted by what might have been and watchful
for what might be still; turned round, as if
my life were in my hands and spilling out,
as if the law of averages had tripped me
one too many times and not enough
to keep my eyes from scanning the horizon—
or like a boy I'd added where I should
subtract and so am made to stay and count
and count. But my mind's not in it.
Not that I'm a fool who stares out windows
sailing ships or slaying dragon clouds
when what's at hand requires my attention.
Yet as if I were a chronic gambler,
it's the winnings of imaginings
I want. God I love that—when they play
without you, safe and sound within your hearing,
forgiving you for thinking of yourself.

On Leash

You watch the forefeet lift and lose all tension.
What art we now require to retrieve
the grace we humans lost in our ascension,
the innocence for which our sinews grieve.
And then the arc from collar to your hand
goes tight—a movement only she can sense
becomes a snarling, leaping dog, unmanned
behind the stroboscopic cedar fence.
Leave it! So. The two of you walk on,
her instinct thwarted by your will and strength,
the leash returning to its proper length—
the forefeet lift, the call to violence gone;
yet there's a remnant at her mouth of foam
that's like the referent loosed inside a poem.

Off Leash

Strolling, with your own dog, maybe, loosed
under the sky and on a green expanse,
you feel your own unbound exuberance,
your spirit, by its wanton leaping, goosed
(the more so that the leash is in your hand)
into a higher realm of happiness:
time, you're sure, however less,
enough for all the foolish things you've planned.
Till like the barking dog behind the fence,
compared to whose constrained intelligence
the comprehension of all human beings
seems vast, you turn toward the bitter leavings
of some gnawed, appalling, savage bone
you buried in a corner all your own.

The News and Ancient Tales

After the news, October 1, 2000—
the father nodding like a broken doll
when the spat of gunning stopped and the white dust settled,
the son no longer screaming for his life
but emptied out and lying still—
we read our book of ancient Chinese tales.
My son read one and I made out the moral,
then I . . . and he . . . then he . . . and I . . . and so
we traded off till several tales were told:
the man whose neighbors, one by one, turned thieves,
until he found his ax just where he'd left it;
the farmer who came home and told his wife
he'd pulled on all their rice to help it grow;
the clam and snipe that wouldn't end their fight
until the fisherman made off with both.

We closed the book, then glancing at the clock,
played piano though I cannot play—
a mad, percussive, father-son duet;
a rite of being where we were and not
in crossfire and camera range against
the white wall of some desert holy site.
And when we said good-night we didn't linger,
for neither of us wanted to be greedy,
and understatement suits us more than prayer—
though in the dark, before he let me go,
he asked obliquely, "What are you going to do?"
and seeing what he meant I answered, "Read."

The Trumpet Vine

That final day, in paradise almost,
my son and I had bathing suits, my daughter
had forgotten hers, but calm, cool water
coaxed her in, in shorts and camisole.

We lay in sun and sand beside the pond
till with her mother's help her things had dried,
and when we wandered to the ocean side
there seemed a widening of the family bond,

for I had seen something my daughter'd showed
her mother—that their huddling in the store,
once we had got what we had come there for,
confirmed. And with our sack of rocky road

in hand, my son and I went out to wait,
his curiosity not quite at rest—
though as for that I think he too had guessed,
yet proved discretion an acquired trait,

for when they came out to the porch, he asked,
as if he had to know, "What's in the bag?"
I could have made a schoolyard joke and rhymed
but held my tongue and kept my pleasure masked.

Then at the trailhead parking lot again
we waited for the two of them and walked

up Prospect Hill, and on the summit talked
about how beautiful our trip had been.

And as we left the insect-clicking woods,
I saw the trumpet vine that made a bower
of that simple hut where from that hour
my daughter'd reached the age of womanhood—

the overtopping vine, the coral flower
signifying earthly life was good.

II.

Jackson Square, New Orleans

Midmorning, as the Tarot cards proceeded,
police removed the dead man from the square.
A bride and groom pulled up, almost unheeded
a juggler tossed his pins into the air.
The general rode his rearing horse above
the palms, magnolias, and flower beds;
a black magician caged and cloaked his dove.
Carriage horses shook their bridled heads;
the groom flung green and purple necklaces
into the crowd; the band went round the corner.
The cage collapsed before few witnesses.
The dead man passed, arms crossed, without a mourner,
looking kingly with his grizzled beard;
above the lamp, the dove had reappeared.

In the Cathedral: Bruckner's *Locus Iste*

Far, far above our heads the tiles were broken—
I wondered when the missing pieces fell
and let my eyes drop straight below to where.
We'd come to hear the winter choral concert—
Bruckner, Brahms, Hovhaness, Duruflé.
Not so much for them; our friends were singing.
We spotted them stage right and farthest left—
bass and soprano in an aging choir
uplifted by an unseen organist.
"This is God's house," the sacred song proclaimed.

The choir in their black gowns and tuxedos
held their black-bound books just slantwise, out
so that the tops of the white pages showed
and made white Vs against the black and black,
like birds you'd draw—or couldn't draw and so
drew Vs—but these were flying, choiring
in silence to the choir's sacred song—
suspended like the crucifix behind them—
coming toward you—stark white gulls at midnight
over a dark or non-existent sea.

Painting

The chair that was his subject hardly mattered.
From his wooden box he chose titanium white,
thalo blue, and cadmium yellow, light—
he saw her rise, he saw the mirror shattered—
selected from the nearly infinite
thalo red, light gray, mars violet,
and cadmium yellow, deep—his palette
balancing the willed and requisite.
And then he turned his gaze back to the chair
that stood for nothing but what wasn't there
and wondered how to paint the air—
the shattered mirror seemingly aware,
within its blue and white titanium,
that every painting is a requiem.

The Mailbox

Every day before the mailman came—
or seeing he must have come and gone by now—
he thought, at last, he wouldn't be the same
but changed—he didn't know exactly how.
As if a magic man would lift his hat,
the children trembling at the magic word,
and then a rabbit would appear—like that!
(Unless the incantation were misheard.)
What was it that he hoped to find in it,
as one who follows hopes to hear a call,
or as a rocking crone might sit and knit
a scarf for one who wouldn't live till fall?
Something printed with the stamp of fact,
addressing what in dwelling there he lacked.

Private Showing

One by one she brought them out to show—
the paintings that in privacy she kept
turned backward in the basement down below
the noisy floors where other people slept.
What to make of it we didn't know

but looked in affirmation at her art,
the way you'd nod when someone candid spoke,
and never fixed on any crooked part
or cast about for some remark or joke,
as if afraid of arguments we'd start.

They seemed the scenes of the subconscious mind,
the forms and colors less of fear than wish,
the central figures never humankind,
a goat, a cock, a donkey, and a fish
in light that seemed a vision of the blind.

And when we saw it there, exposed and tense—
the part of her that no one else had seen—
we wondered if we'd earned such confidence,
or if our being there had turned obscene
the thing that in her solitude made sense.

The Last Dryad

Once long ago he did a crazy thing.
What brought it back—the rainy summer night
or a waiting, inward reckoning
that cast his motives in a later light?
It wasn't only physically perverse
but seemed to take a philosophic turn—
a mythic scene an actor might rehearse
or goldsmith hammer on a dead man's urn
to dramatize the tragic strain in man.
A death wish—that's what his friend had said.
Though he'd have called himself a charlatan,
who tried to rouse what wasn't even dead:
fingering from behind the lifeless eyes,
the cold wet bronze, the sculptured breasts and thighs.

On Seeing *Monster's Ball*

What a part that other actress played!
She walked into the room, took off her blouse
and then her skirt, and turned about, legs splayed,
as Sonny played the master of the house.
Not that he stood more dignified than she,
but he had other scenes and other acts
to win the audience's sympathy—
a life that went beyond the so-called facts.
I guess I didn't mention she was paid
and had a line about her being sore.
There is an art, of course, to either trade,
and which of us is not, at times, a whore?
Her business was the shock of recognition—
we play along who only pay admission.

The Chinese Princess Tree

Every afternoon on days they teach
they meet beneath the Chinese princess tree
to underscore their prominence, each to each,
commuting misery to company.
Pretty girls—the good ones keep their distance—
smile at their avuncular advances,
while boys who like to talk of Marx, for instance—
the kind who sneer at soccer games and dances—
honor them and raise their share of smoke,
as if they, too, stood high above their peers;
bringing to the table one more joke
to prove their masculinity and years.
And no one but the princess tree's alert
to the smoke in its branches and the butts in its dirt.

Still Life

Each discipline had left him cold.
With every form came restlessness.
Nothing lasted. His Ph.D.
had landed him a job—no more.
What he was he was in dreams,
and these he had in fits and starts.
What others meant by love and spirit
he knew by intimation only,
as when an object turned to still life—
the marble, the pencil and its shadow—
and sounds—the ticking clock, the traffic—
to the markers of a constant silence
—or when his wife was gone.
So that the thing that made him human—
his consciousness, his practiced sense
that he could say of things, *As if*—
had only made him wonder more
what living could have been without it.

Art Form

To hell with words, he said, and put a rock
atop a rock—or had he come across
these roughhewn columns? Block on block,
an art form purged of dross,
austere, exact; a world without debris,
beautiful, and out-of-doors:
the steely gray of glacial scree,
the rusted purple of the moors—
as if he'd landed there, as having flown
unguided save by some prophetic sight,
looking down to where he might alight,
then dropping to his own two feet, alone
but for the friend still hovering in the air,
whose metamorphosis had got him there.

Major American Authors I

Nine bells. So sings the coffin-maker, time.
I will not count—yet in an hour I will
stand chalky as a corpse against the blackboard,
not dead but like the man behind the blindfold
waiting, my only cigarette a perfect
cylinder that in its former forms
housed living beings beneath a living sea.
A quarter past—the halls are empty, quiet—
the water pipes and Coke machines at ease.
Not that they hate me—they don't—at times
we even laugh or speak as if to thee
and thou, at times are even moved to silence.
There's the half hour—I have a page to read,
notes to overlook. Outside, the day is gray,
the pigeons whirl, the stones of Midwest Gothic
architecture look their part; more leaves
will fall and snow will finish the picture.
The bells redouble as the hour diminishes.
"A quarter hour yet . . . then I'll not be."
That's next semester. Today's Thoreau's conclusion,
the Kouroo artist who would not let time enter
in the making of his perfect staff—
Where're my notes? Too late, the hammer strikes.
Like Quentin I descend the dusty steps,
thinking of Cash—"the Chuck. Chuck. Chuck. of the adze."
Yet even as I fold my arms, the present
seeps like water through the beveled joints

and happily I come across the line—
"Time is but the stream I go a-fishing in."

III.

The Gray House

Just days before the move and the divorce,
in the mirror we carried flat like a table top—
the open not the boarded surface upward—
our house reversed and in strange angles from
below (far below the floor, it seemed),
the ceiling, walls, and windows shuddered, tumbling
as we tapped our way downstairs from our parents' bedroom
to the first floor landing, and down the basement steps.
We couldn't help but laugh, my brother and I,
the funny house between us, though we felt
the edge and weight of that wide sheet of glass
and what our mother asked of us, her sons.
And as we laughed the tumbling got worse:
the house-fragmented glass kaleidoscoped
and I grew dizzy and dizzier—as if
with one more step I'd be inside it. "Don't look!"
my brother cried, "Don't look at it! Don't look!"
foreseeing the mad descent that could have followed.
It was no accident—I let it drop
to make the floor come back, the tumbling stop.

Stick Figure

She told the kids, "This is a game—a test,"
and getting paper had them draw a man.
She's not supposed to tell us why, he guessed,
and since he liked to draw he just began.
He made a pirate with a sword and gun,
an eye patch, then a parrot on one shoulder.
His sister drew five lines and then was done—
"Go on, don't stop!" he should have told her.
The minute up, he put his pencil down,
and if their drawings didn't tell the tale,
their mother did. "Wow!" she said—then frowned
and giving back his sister's said, "You fail!"
It seemed his sister's self-esteem was lacking,
nor did he offer it the pirate's backing.

The Sailor and the Actor

I.

Given what we lived on wasn't much,
we didn't need the Herman Miller couch,
the Dali and Picasso lithographs.
The table where we ate and had such laughs
was not the sort at which one put on airs,
especially while the Mirskys screamed upstairs.
Someday, of course, we hoped he'd come along,
the man she loved, and he'd be big and strong
and free her from her secretary's salary:
all our birthday wishes were she'd marry.
You'd not believe the odd discrepancies
between her wishes and realities:
the riding lessons and the live-in maid
who shared my sister's room the year she stayed;
the sailor, a photographer, who drove
an Aston Martin and made love,
she told us, better even than the actor,
whose genius wrestled with some human factor;
the neighborhood from which we'd not be saved
by flights up Mulholland—so something gave
about each month or so, in rough proportion
to the luxury she thought her truer portion.
And thus we learned, in incongruity
and other ways, our mom's humanity.

II.

I learned our father's differently—in court:

43

he stood across the aisle, before the judge
and all the other witnesses, and cried.
We three had taken sides from early on
and I, in judge's chambers, said as much.
It was our mother brought him there—for money.
She wanted more, we thought that he had plenty—
had seen his signs, our common name,
on real estate along commercial streets,
and in his bathroom cabinet other signs
revealed to us he'd more or less remarried.
And now, alone in court, defending himself—
fool for a client, foolish advocate—
he told the judge his boy (I couldn't recall
him calling me that ever) said to him
our mother only let us have one egg
for breakfast—for so she'd half-decreed,
half-kidding, then put us up to blaming him.
Breaking runnily himself now, glasses off.
And I believe that was what swayed the judge
against her—her devices ever failing.

III.
Though once there was a man who took us sailing
in the moonlight through the harbor out to sea,
where other sailboats passed like apparitions,
and we shared our mother's fantasy.
Till on the dock, behind me, from his shoulders,
my sister asked him, "Could you be our father?"
To which he said at last, "Of course I could!"
And then we drove back to West Hollywood.

Show's Over

Afterward, she realized the freezer
had an automatic, timed defrost
and that it wasn't us at all who'd left her
water where she wanted ice.
But now at dinnertime, or just before,
she asked us, Who's been using all the ice?
and when we answered, each in turn, Not me,
she went crazy—literally, I mean.
Her eyes went back into her head, her neck
turned red, the veins bulged out, she screamed and screamed
as if she'd taken leave of who she was
and something else possession of her soul.
We tried to calm her down, to get her back—
this mother who had worked all day, we knew,
and whom we owed more than we could provide;
we tried to tell her, "It's all right," and I
stood up and held her by the shoulders
till her eyes came down and all her rage subsided
and she fixed on me that *Et tu, Brutè?* look.
The next day she said she was only playing—
as an actress would—for sympathy,
or therapy; she knew what she was doing.
But if it worked for her, for us it backfired.
We treated her with care, it's true; but from
that moment on it was every man for himself.

Young Sophocles

Home from school, for some forgotten reason,
half an hour before my younger sister,
it struck me I'd commit a sort of treason
against our mom, who played the part of Mr.

and worked full-time, giving us the household run,
and was always threatening suicide
and having fits because we hadn't done
the dishes, or wouldn't take her side

against our father—or our grandmother
who robbed her of her personality;
a bastard and a slob she called the other.
What crime (she'd ask) had made her life so shitty?

Though a beauty, her beauty stayed unsung
except by men who sang and went away—
a sailor and an actor, neither young,
who didn't really want a divorcée.

—As I said, to commit blasphemy
against the dread that ruled our childhood,
perform a matricidal tragedy
that left no trace of sanctity or blood,

I hung her wig and robe and slippers from
the fixture in the center of the ceiling,

its back toward the doorway of her room,
then hid across the hallway almost reeling

when my sister, thinking no one home,
turned and stared, then saw it wasn't mom
and screamed—in horror you'd assume,
but it was like the lifting of our doom.

The Hitchhiker

Once traveling in my father's Cadillac—
an Eldorado, ancient history—
my brother, younger sister, me in back,

we asked a man in uniform if he
could tell us where to go, for we were lost.
My father's friend was with us, too, and she

stared straight ahead, as if directions cost
much more than any foreigner could pay
(distrust the boundary she had never crossed).

I guess the soldier was on holiday.
Bespectacled, his hair buzz-cut, he said
he'd gladly ride with us and show the way—

the turn was just a mile or so ahead.
Have I said yet he was hitchhiking?
It was a common sort of childhood dread—

our father at some restaurant asking,
with menu spread, as if he owned the place,
for something that the waitress couldn't bring.

But this was worse, and worse still, to save face
he blamed his closed-door policy on us;
the sun descending on the desert base.

I wanted to get out and take a bus
or take my stand beside all stranded men;
the hopeful soldier now incredulous

at seeing the Caddy climb the ramp again—
and in me, too, some filial thing gone.

In the L.A. Half-Light

Because my father fell and broke his hip
I missed the game. No matter, my friend Mat
had tickets for the next night too—way up
in the upper deck; it's lucky we were fit—
we climbed a thousand stairs. The surgery'd
gone well that afternoon. The day before
we waited hours in emergency
for X-rays and the orthopedic doctor.
It's funny how you get to know your dad
again—when he is failing, as they say;
pretty soon you know he will be dead—
then you'll know him still another way.
The mountains lovely as they'd ever been
above the lights, the crowd, the night-game green.

Diamond

Home, first, second, third, the pitcher's mound,
the infield dirt, the grass, the warning track,
the wall, the foul poles, and the crowd spellbound,
the cityscape and sky that take you back;
the wind-up and the pitch and then the crack
and echoing of something more profound
than ball and bat, an aphrodisiac
of movement, specificity, and sound;
the physical suspense by which we're bound
and braced, like passenger to paperback,
to watch the center fielder cover ground
and make up any passages we lack
of happiness or wholesomeness or love
until the ball comes down into his glove.

Notes for the Rabbi's Eulogy

"My condolences," the rabbi said
by telephone to each of us in turn—
and so, as prearranged, we went ahead
to help the rabbi learn
about the father and the widow's groom—
in what had been his living room

in Santa Monica,
the ocean just a parking lot away;
the mirrored shelves on which his second wife
had placed the souvenirs they'd bought on trips
from Iceland to Antarctica
before they both required replacement hips
(that recently acquired souvenir
that would outlast him even in the grave);
the balcony from which as kids we watched
the fireworks shot from the pier,
and where a later day
he'd watch for us and wave
in that peculiar, nervous, loving way

—so that the rabbi's eulogy
might voice our father's personality:

how trumpeting his cheeks he'd play the trumpet
trumpetless, and when we'd ask him,
"What are we going to do today?"
chafing more with boredom year by year,

he'd say, "Play it by ear,"
or else he'd sing, "O solo mio,"
adding lyrically, "My name is Leo"—
all those Saturdays when without fail
(however late the check was in the mail),
first in the Opal, then the Cadillac,
first singly, then with one we'd never call
our own, though always she kept coming back,
and in whose living room at last we sat—
he'd take us somewhere:
Griffith park, the Planetarium
to watch the pegs knocked by the pendulum,
roasting hot dogs after that,
or to the Safeway and his bachelor flat
on Los Feliz—
we weren't hard to please:
each with his turkey or his chicken pie,
Tubby the Tuba on the hi-fi,
or Brigadoon—
till all that ended much too soon

for us, who could not measure once a week
his loneliness, or hers, come round,
"O solo mio" in the dim background,
of which the rabbi would soon speak.

Identification

To look more would have been for art's sake,
like some data hound;
death takes the place of privacy—
you want the curtain down.

Eyes closed—as only children can
be innocently viewed;
something deformed about the mouth
—no child and past a man.

Serious, alert,
as in the picture of him at my wedding
tucking in his shirt,
though motionless and unselfconscious

—cold.
I put my hand down on his shoulder,
the comfortable wool of his tuxedo—
not his marble skin.

The rest is history,
things everybody knows—
Ecclesiastes and Psalm 23,
the rabbi and the dirt.

The Cabinetmaker

Something about a dresser he'd converted
to a desk—our father whom I'd never known
to put his hand to any workman's task—
our uncle, who had known him as a boy,
weeping in the telling at the lectern:
the pine coffin right, the mound of dirt
covered by a green tarp, the rose of Sharon
and the L.A. sky above the gentle roar
of traffic, not unlike the roar he lived by
five miles away in Santa Monica.

All these years that desk had signified
his older brother's know-how and persistence,
his will to educate himself and rise
above their immigrant, illiterate parents—
our grandfather a baker till he halved
the thumb whose nub-end I remember (from when
he squeezed the siphon's trigger-valve in Brooklyn).
And with the wife and child of his old age
beside him now, our uncle, blowing his nose,
read out the speech he'd typed as eulogy:
a businessman's biography, as if
of some great man, his partner here survived
to tell us so—weeping since he, too,
identified the stranger in the coffin.

Next to us our father's second wife
but only widow, I suppose—his first

would have the three of us for dinner later—
endured the eulogy till it was over.
And then our father's sister spoke; then I.
I thanked his friends for coming, one of whom
had also known our father as a boy,
and told them he'd have liked to talk with them,
for I could picture that, and said we'd all
find ways to talk with him; that it was good
to learn new things about him—how much I'd liked
the story of the dresser and the desk.

And then the rabbi wrapped things up—and we,
and those behind us, all who wanted to,
dropped dirt down on the pine wood box to put
the finish on the cabinetmaker's work.

The Boy's Hand on the Hill

"Come, my Captain. Study out the course,
and let us away! See, see! the boy's face from
the window! The boy's hand on the hill!"
— Starbuck to Ahab

Down from the Holiday Inn—the traffic signal
piping for the blind like Melville's *Rachel* sweeping
the horizon for its missing children—
under the arch of Santa Monica Pier:
"YACHT HARBOR, SPORT FISHING, BOATING, Cafés,"
past the cocktail palms, the sleeping men,
the cannon I remember straddling
one Saturday some forty years ago
(the day I mocked my father's splayfoot gait),
I walk the ramp that bridges Highway 1
to the pier, the trodden wood, the carousel—
the promenade that in the early morning
leaves me to my thoughts (in May I saw
a threesome, *muy borracho*, trading off
a dangling rubber phallus); this morning mine
between tomorrow's hillside ceremony
and the unfamiliar gathering yesterday.

I keep my eye as best I can on one
green drifting spot through which the movement in
the water passes—the wave the spirit
only seen in matter rising, falling
left behind its breaking. So images

of my father and his phrases pass through thoughts
that float and drift like refuse and debris.
A circus is in town, its vast white tent
a cityscape of conic peaks and flags
that will be struck again and disappear;
the real cityscape—the cliff and clock
and concrete bridge—I've known since childhood.
Ahead I see the rounding Ferris wheel,
the pier foreshortened and the wide horizon,
a line of pelicans, a swooping gull
when through me comes the sense of panorama—
the independence that was what he wanted
most of me and in me most esteemed;
my father's whole and broken fatherhood
upwelling, distancing my walking on.

In my pocket two clay shards, two rounded stones;
the shards from where I met my wife, the stones
from God knows where—I used to know.
That day he handed me the lawyer's card—
"Because you're interested," he said (prepared,
he meant, to think about the fact of death)—
the day before he broke his hip and spiraled
up and down from floor to floor, yet months
before sarcoma ended him, hands poised
and pale atop the Lexus steering wheel,
he said he wished they'd save their resources
for young people and lay him warrior-like
in his canoe and cast him out to sea.
He lived in the first of those white towers down shore.

Deep water below us, the sun already hot,
a fisherman folds up his phone and asks me
if I'll watch his poles so he can change to shorts.
And having earned then something in return,
I ask him what he's fishing for and if
he'd any luck, taking from his answer only
"baitfish," a word that somehow pleases me.
And then I pass more fishermen with dark
and darker skin and stop where I can go
no farther, nothing past the rail but water
and the rocking of the buoy bell—that clangs
and clangs again and then not now.
I watch the sun rays slanting toward the piles
in water green and see-through to the flashing
baitfish down below—whole schools of them—
and wonder what big fish they're luring in.
A man walks to the rail and slices one
from gill to tail then drops it accidentally,
cursing as he walks away. A boy
goes bucket-laden to the sink. Two lovers
come and speak in Spanish; nuzzling her
he whispers and she tosses back her head
and laughs. The buoy sways and clangs.

My hand is in my pocket now—to the left
the water-slapping wings of a cormorant
and overhead a calling "kirikak."
One shard, one stone I'm saving for a spot
just down the beach my father took me to—
a T-shaped boardwalk ending in the sand

where he would come and make his stand, as if
against Indifferent Immortality.
"What brings men to the sea?" he asked. Another
of Ishmael's water gazers, I tried to say.
Then in the lobby of Casa del Mar
he drank green tea and chatted with the waitress
in the manner of all Brooklyn-born old men;
I preferred his company and Guinness
and through the gorgeous windows watched the sea.
Today, I think, I'll end my morning there.
But now I throw the stone and shard, first one
and then the other, far beyond the pier—
as if to where the waves will carry them
not in but out, as if he were in them
in his canoe—although I know they'll sink
in darkness there below the sounding buoy.

Turning then, I see the strangest thing:
a pigeon with one foot not there—
the knobby leg a pulpy red and white
reminding me of something. What?
And then it comes to me—a lollipop,
the sucking done, the cherry candy gone.
Poor pigeon though; he looks at me like some
old peg-legged captain, hardly Ahab-like—
as if his cruel loss hadn't made him thoughtful
and he had wasted it on crumbs. And yet
his eye still seems a sort of magic glass.
We'd both gone to the pier's end to report:
"And I only am escaped alone to tell thee."

IV.

That Stranger

No one's alone these days. People are nervous,
nervous! You see them walking with their arms
crooked—in some obligatory service
meant to check or mitigate alarms.
Big Brother of an oddly-ringing sort
that like the Devil hides in a disguise:
a friendly chat or cynical retort,
the notion that to keep in touch is wise.
But I'm afraid it only makes things worse,
like any crutch—without it now you're lost;
a modern, liberated sort of curse:
you pay much more than what you thought it cost—
your self-reliance and your introspection,
that stranger who'd have asked for some direction.

Against the Backdrop of the Great Façade

Harlaxton Manor, Lincolnshire

The stranger here, I walk with deference—
they warned us Saturday of Monday shoots;
the jeeps parked down the lane make perfect sense
as do the men with guns and rubber boots.
Three of them along the red brick wall
tramp north beyond the gardener's residence
toward the woods. A white dog and a black
run out until they hear their masters call—
and then, like caroms on a string, run back.

Just at the crossing of the road for goods
I ask a man if it is pheasants that
they're after. "Yes." He points. "We'll push the woods
in that direction"—smiling as we chat.
"You should be safe enough." He seems to know
with airy confidence like Robin Hood's
I'm with the Yankee college at the manor.
Three more approach along the hawthorn row,
more workmanlike in outfitting and manner,

the middle one now doubled up because
his Labrador has got herself a rabbit,
in answer to her own unmannered laws,
drops it on command for him to grab it,

requiring no fanfare or reward,
nor gentle strokes or soft hurrahs—
pacing now as if to go again;
whereat the stocky man who is her lord
uplifts the rabbit by the hind legs and

knocks it with the barrel of his gun,
fouling off the limply swinging head,
then raising it to get it squarely done
so that the rabbit knows it's dead.
He slips it deftly ears-first in his inner
pocket, hiding what he's won,
folds the hind legs so they're tucked away;
to his friends exclaiming, "That's me dinner!"
—one for which he didn't have to pay.

Although the way he doesn't look at me,
as if I were the master of the land,
suggests that fear and culpability
are this man's fare, whatever comes to hand.
Unless because he seems to count me out
and makes no nod as I walk by,
though I would like to take a passing share,
I read into his countenance some doubt
where nothing but his disregard is there.

Blind Man on a Night's Walk

I won't forget his television eyes
or how he stood there with his blind man's cane.
It's hard to separate the truth from lies.

Lost, as from across the Bridge of Sighs,
he heard me, called to me, his voice urbane—
the lamplight on his opalescent eyes.

A man does what he can and should—he tries.
The Bishop stops and talks to Crazy Jane,
but can he separate the truth from lies?

How many things we artfully disguise!
How many ways our charity is vain!
Up close I shuddered at his sci-fi eyes.

And who among us won't prioritize?
And did he live then on a higher plane
the while he handed me a pack of lies?

I gave him cash, a ride home—was it wise
or was I playing Abel to his Cain?
I won't forget his television eyes.
It's hard to separate the truth from lies.

An Old Photo on Today's Front Page

Immediately you see it's out of date:
a black and white—the Whirlpool Bldg. blurred,
two striking workers, Local 808.
The thing that calls to you, without a word,
is not the subject, not the time and place
specifically—but just the past
that comes across in coats, a worker's face,
and in the medium, the poor contrast.
You know you were alive when it was taken,
twenty years—or not so long—ago;
you feel a former sense of things awaken,
perceiving how the paper used to show
life's graininess, its winter weather gray—
not half so colorful as life today.

The Painters

Two painters in white shirts and overalls
sit side by side before the slide and swings,
their legs bent at the knees, their backs upright—
like the tread and risers of a back-door step—
white against a field of mostly green.
They've turned their heads to watch a child swinging,
or else to watch its California mother—
what they're watching isn't in the picture:
you see the grass, the concrete tunnel, blue,
the redwood bench that runs the other way,
crossing them, foreshortened, weathered gray.

The tree that's at the head of it, a linden,
shades the front end of the painters' truck—
tail-gate down, tarps folded, silver cans
stacked up, a ladder racked above its bed—
that blocks the open door of the apartment
whose dark interior they're painting white.
They look like cutouts in a color canvas,
a painting that they painted centerward,
themselves the only part that's left undone.
Until they rise to finish off their work,
the painting painted and the painters gone.

The Balloon-Blower

He blew so hard it seemed about to burst,
swelling like the belly of a glutton,
a little innocent, a little cursed,
then took his mouth away and tied the button,
having recognized its proper station,
whose membrane anyone could come and tap
or prick, according to his inclination—
a gift he'd offer to the gods of hap,
knowing that if it broke it was part air
and that the other part would hardly matter,
it wouldn't hurt to see it stranded there—
though as for that he liked it better fatter;
for though its form was something preconceived,
it wasn't anything until he breathed.

The Rakers

He raked on—grandpa with his infant helper
tricycling around as I walked by,
somewhat in the middle, though nearer the elder—
we nodded as we caught each other's eye.
The word that came to mind was "Neverending,"
but that's just what it isn't. However young
the rakers, however old and bending,
however many plastic necks are wrung
and baggy bodies sentenced to the dump,
however choked the drains and blocked the gutters
winter blankly comes in spades to trump
the fall, and all its mad descending sputters
and is finally finished—and one by one
the rakers' raking's done.

A Voice Out of the Blue

Pedaling on my bicycle I passed him
as he pushed his electric mower up the walk
between the knot of ivy and his house
and into the shade of his midsummer maple:
hunched in his jumpsuit, bald, his shoulders slumped,
an old car buff—Caddies and Chevrolets
he fixed in his garage and sold to the faithful.
"Hi-ya, Vern," I called, just barely slowing.

But he didn't seem to hear, pushing on,
flat as a cardboard cutout from behind.
I could have pedaled by but called again,
"Hi, Vernon." And then he stopped, looked left,
and held dead still, as if he'd heard a voice—
as if an angel or a ghost had called him
and the earth had gone a turn without him—
and even then I could have left him stranded.

"Hi, Vern"—I used my brakes—"just saying hello!"
He quickly turned and waved a hand, "Hi-there!"
—then tucked the end in of the mower's cord
as I pedaled round the corner. Crossing Lincoln,
I looked a second long at two men walking—
one seemed familiar, though I couldn't place him—
then looking left I saw I'd crossed too soon,
and then it hit me—just as the car did

(I seemed myself to hold an instant still

and could have counted all the cars approaching
and the fat green leaves of the cottonwood)—
that Vernon's turn to a voice out of the blue
had not been a mistake but seconds early,
not age so much as premonition.
How strange he was the one I thought of last—
an old man I said hello to as I passed.

Tractor

In the field the tractor goes
slowly up and down the rows,

red and green with upright bearing
over the horizon faring

like a ship on deep brown earth,
tires of enormous girth

clotted with the giving ground,
coming with the time around

(calligraphic water glints
where coots had left their icy prints:

wind and sunlight correspond—
picturesque, the field and pond).

Landscape and the human factor:
from the bridge you watch the tractor.

V.

The Tomb of Hunting and Fishing

In the Tomb of Hunting and Fishing, Tarquinia,
a hunter stands mid-motion on a rock,
the slingshot stretched these two millennia,
the nearest bird about to take the shock;
while in the boat two boys, their arms outspread,
signal to the oarsman, worn away,
that fish—this big—are jumping dead ahead,
although the angler, bowed, could wait all day.
The birds fly off in two and three directions,
arcing upward over the painting's border,
as from below the dolphins' resurrections
mirror their curving dives and make an order
less of nature's than the painter's art—
though in the short run nature played its part.

National Veterans Creative ARTS Festival

for Michael Naranjo

He met the Pope and touched the marble David.
He was Disabled Veteran of the Year,
blinded by a hand grenade in Viet Nam,
his right hand permanently maimed. A sculptor:
hoop and eagle dancers, warriors, hunters—
dark and without eyes, the way he sees them.
Above our kitchen sink's a bear he made,
its forelegs bent and lifted, head turned back,
a heavy little bronze he named "Sniff, Sniff."

He taught me how to fish—to tie a swivel
fast to a line, and how to cast and reel
with Kastmasters and Super-Dupers, spoons,
and floats and flies, small browns and Pistol Petes
—like a reaper in slow motion, backwards.
With his teeth and fingers he'd untangle knots
I made or stand and hold the hook-end
as I walked back through the trees to loose the line.
He'd imitate a crow to near perfection.
And taught me, too, to jerk the line against
a hit, then reel it in and swing the fish
over the sedge and dirt, and grab it in
one hand, unclip the clip and thread it through
the gill and mouth, then drop the fish and chain

into the shallow, muddied water.

One daughter played the harp; the other danced
to mariachi music in the plaza.
We'd stand for hours, drink a beer or two
beneath the mountain he called Tsikumuu,
where he'd hunted elk and deer with his father and brother.
When the rangers came, he'd shoot the shit with them
in Tewa—sometimes get me out of paying.
And by the summer's end we'd catch our share
and lose some, too—just at the sedge they'd jump
and twist and flip, we'd feel the line go slack
and watch them dart into the darker green.
From the mouths of the baby trout we'd disengage
the treble hooks or smaller flies, then hold
the water round them till they'd wake and vanish.

But the fat ones, the firm and heavy ones,
long since they'd settled, dying on the chain,
we'd clean downstream; and that he taught me too—
to hold the fish turned down, thumb in the gill,
and pierce the hole above the tail and upward
slit the flesh, unzipping it, then cut
the tendon, plucking out the jellied guts
and in one motion slinging them across
the stream for what would come and find them—bears,
he said, or coyotes. Back along the road
he'd ask politely if the coast was clear,
then on the long ride home we'd talk about
his operations to remove the shrapnel

from his upper spine and stop the leak of fluid
in his skull; and his crazy sisters, my wife's five aunts,
her mother, and her half-brother's divorce;
about our marriages, and raising kids;
the fishing trip he planned to Mexico;
and his sculptures—the shows he had upcoming.

I have a long-sleeved denim shirt he gave me,
an extra-large, too large for both of us,
he got for free in Washington, D.C.,
the only thing I wear that bears the colors—
red, white, and blue in a patch above the pocket
beside the lettering in black that names
the festival that it commemorates:
National Veterans Creative ARTS.
The stripes are lines in a plowed and hilly field,
the stars are in the sky, just where they should be,
and to the right's a palette, a treble clef,
a dancer, and the mask of comedy.

Down East on the 4th

Americans will kill themselves
    in folding-chairs on bridges,
or slowly make it home to die
    on opening their fridges:

the boats gone by, their cigarettes
    and fireworks gone off,
the TV on, the sound turned up—
    the rattle and the cough.

There was a house right on the road,
    "Beware of Dog," it said;
its shutters shut, a man came out
    to prove he wasn't dead.

He met some friends to square his life
    of alcoholic squalor;
"Good 4th," they said to us, polite
    as portraits on a dollar.

We ate our pancakes in a church,
    plain and wild blueberry.
Across the seas the Japanese
    and South Korean ferry

stayed in port while missiles went—
    and we, the innocent,

tried to guess what Washington
    and North Korea meant.

We had a lunch of salmon smoked
    across from Schoodic Point
in Grindstone where the wealthy stay
    and nothing's out of joint.

We took a 9.8-mile walk,
    thanks to Conservancies
that think the world's a better place
    reserved for vacancies.

How far we had to travel for
    the fog-obscured horizon,
the lobster boats and pine islands
    and what we kept our eyes on—

bald eagles hunting eider down
    chicks barely in first-feather.
Ah, nature—rude—awakening
    at last to lovely weather!

How valiantly the mother rose
    against the eagle's dive;
the last we saw, out of the three,
    one chick was still alive.

They went behind the island rocks
    joined by a faithful few,

but there the eagles went as well,
    relentlessly on cue.

Then all that summer afternoon
    our naked eyes discerned
up in the pines a spot of white
    investing what it earned.

And to our question—did they get them
    all?—that spot replied.
(It was in our binoculars
    death framed and magnified:

not cruel, nor kind, but decent, worthy
    —sort of Lincolnesque.)
We wondered if the end of man
    would look so picturesque.

Stray

I woke in the place I knew myself to be,
and there, in the doorway to the balcony,
I saw the dog I'd left behind, now dead
and in that phantom state attentive to
my wish to follow and my holding back.
He turned and left the room deliberately,
as if to say your coming's up to you,
unmastered by the will I seemed to lack.
And though I must have been asleep in bed,
I feared as much the breaking of the spell
as its immortal paradise or hell.
Should I have risen, gone with him outside
before I let my consciousness subside—
or looking backward then would I have died?

Leave Taking

for Louis Owens

A suicide, he sat his motorcycle—
white, with an empty sidecar—and looked at me
from halfway down the dark, suburban street.
Right-angled in a driveway, on another
motorcycle—white, with an empty sidecar—
a companion waited: a man I did not know.

He taught me how to read *The Sound and the Fury*,
to hold the Canticle of St. Francis—
Brother Sun and Sister Moon—against
Macbeth—the walking shadow, dusty death.
He never had a motorcycle sidecar,
though, like Quentin, must have had a sister—

one of nine children, born to migrant workers—
and in a novel searched for his brother's bones
in a riverbed—a story that he knew
but couldn't change. Part Cherokee and Choctaw,
part not, he took it all to heart—big heart,
eyes like Charles Bronson's, an athlete.

He took it to heart all right, the way you'd take it
to the hole, in the airport parking lot, early,
by his car: solo, grounded—so.
That's where he shot himself not where he died.

"Call it a day, I wish they might have said"—
the lines that play on in a teacher's head.

He taught me racquetball: fifteen to two,
then four, then twelve—jumping jacks, he said,
were good as stretching; and now before I play
I do a hundred in his memory.
And his word in a corridor changed the course of my life.
Then he, my former teacher, made a U-turn

and in the deafening roar rode off,
the other following where I could not,
into the darkness of the street. And I,
on waking, saw that all we know, we know
in symbols, darkly—taking this last lesson
from him even as he took his leave.

Prophecy

After the seminars and freshman labs,
the complimentary strokes and gentle jabs,
the Great Books and the preceptorials,
the weddings, grandchildren, and burials,
Plato's dialogues and Euclid's laws,
the rough-and-ready hammers, chisels, saws,
the rain clouds and the canyon and the lakes
of alternating terms and summer breaks—
his childhood fear of doctors finished him,
the prostate cancer diagnosed too late.
For sixty years his childhood lived in him
to hide that other thing that lay in wait.
All that learning, all that building, naught
but subterfuge to keep from getting caught.

After Death

Standing as he stood those final days,
or in the weeks before them, decimated
by his illness, in a dying haze
that left him open and humiliated,
still on speaking terms with most of us,
though stiff and sideways like a matador,
as if our next move might be devious
and he could tell what we were waiting for,
he reappeared in my nocturnal vision,
unchanged, as we'd grown used to seeing him,
as if between the worlds were no division
and nothing happened in the interim.
Was it selfish that I wondered then—
did this mean he would have to die again?

Companion

All that talk of dying gone from him—
the existential truth of it was all
he'd left. He lay back down and closed his eyes.
We talked around him, watched the curled and nodding
hand he said was coloring—
waking from what we supposed a dream.
"What are you coloring?" one of us asked,
but something came between us and his answer.
I guess it was the cancer.
Though just as well it could have been the phone
or someone getting up to pour the water.

A sort of dog you couldn't call
or whistle to or tell to sit up pretty
sprawling there at everybody's feet,
that wouldn't rise for anyone but him.
It's what we like in dogs: their loyalty,
the fact they're yours, however ornery,
their snoring and their bloodshot eyes, their sighs—
the fact they're waiting, too.
Life is attentiveness amid the boredom,
the sounds that tell us where our masters are.
We watched it as he led it off to bed.

The Juggling of Sympathy

The others grieve—but being family
you're free to treat death realistically.
Whatever time of day they feel is right
they call as if to prove their second sight—
they fear their silence would seem disregard;
to be the real mourner's not so hard.
When all is said mortality's a fact,
but once-removed no one knows how to act.
Of course you try to put them at their ease;
you're quick to say "God bless you!" when they sneeze.
It's odd—this juggling of sympathy,
these arcing gestures, missing civilly.
What kindness tosses through the world of men!
That Death's a hell of a Comedian!

Grief

Not disappointing, just pedestrian—
a feeling you might have after a show
that had the dignity of being done
and didn't really need a standing O.
They're too expected anyhow these days,
as if the characters were each King Lear
in all these wretched musicals and plays—
no wonder men prefer ballgames and beer.
Death authors no climactic act.
Just as the phrase that came into my head
in sideways seeing the car running the red
was *Shit, I'm going to hit it*—matter-of-fact—
You can turn that fan off's the last thing he said
and grief to me the feeling *Damn, he's dead.*

The Wreck

Robin Hood's Bay, Yorkshire

Turning from the rock, I saw the wreck
another hundred yards down cliff and shore:
hull rusted red, uptilted on its side—
too high for any tide
to lift it from the rocks and take it back—
iron-still above the North Sea's roar.

As if a gift, or manageable loan,
it seemed reprieve from thoughts of something ended—
this walk from rock to rock to some addition,
in itself perdition,
picturesque for no eyes but my own;
its life-in-death, by my advance, extended.

To make a sketch I took out pen and pad,
half-thinking of that damned librarian
who in his shelter had survived the Bomb
and in that godless calm
felt blessed by all the reading time he had;
but just as in *The Twilight Zone* that man

in reaching forward saw his glasses drop
and shatter there among the thousand books,
so I, just when the boat-wreck made me think,
ran out of ballpoint ink.

Replacing then my stony writing prop,
I gave up everything but firsthand looks:

H446, the Union Jack back-flying,
the shark-mouthed gash athwart the rusted hull,
the door through which I saw the spell-cast brain,
the drooping gear-shaft chain—
the consecrating waterfall, the crying
cliffward of an angry, bent-necked gull.

And then I thought about the rising tide
and of the small green pen I'd left the sea,
used up, abandoned as the broken shells,
the tales no dead man tells,
and ran, lest I be cut off there beside
the wreck—the hero of some Irony.

Mackerel on a Plate, 1951-52

Tate, St. Ives

Open-mouthed in death, the mackerel—
its outline black, its side scraped white and gray—
eclipsed a whiter plate, elliptical
against the dark brown table; lapis eye
half-ringed in yellow; depthless as
an icon of the 13th century—
the background cobalt blue, scarred by canvas;
paint oily, thick as the ichthyic sea.

I lingered like a haunted art critic,
then joined my family in the Tate café;
the ochre-lichened roofs and pale Atlantic
of the Celtic Sea, the wharf, the Cornish sky,
things that we'd remember all our lives—
the windows and the mackerel at St. Ives.

Arthur Brown's poems have appeared in *Poetry, Michigan Quarterly Review, Southwest Review, Measure, The Malahat Review, Dogwood, The Formalist*, and other journals. His poem "The Tomb of Hunting and Fishing" was selected by William Logan as the winner of the 2005 Morton Marr Poetry Prize and his poem "Jackson Square, New Orleans" won the Nebraska Shakespeare Festival Anne Dittrick Sonnet-Writing Contest. His one-act play "Augustina" was selected by Horton Foote as the winner of the 1999 *Arts & Letters* Drama Prize.

After degrees at the University of California, Berkeley, and the University of New Mexico, Arthur Brown completed his Ph.D. in English at the University of California, Davis. He is currently a professor of literature and creative writing at the University of Evansville.

Printed in the United States
126946LV00004B/34/P